Stadiums and Coliseums

Carla Mooney

Rourke
Educational Media

rourkeeducationalmedia.com

Before Reading:

Building Academic Vocabulary and Background Knowledge

Before reading a book, it is important to tap into what your child or students already know about the topic. This will help them develop their vocabulary, increase their reading comprehension, and make connections across the curriculum.

1. *Look at the cover of the book. What will this book be about?*
2. *What do you already know about the topic?*
3. *Let's study the Table of Contents. What will you learn about in the book's chapters?*
4. *What would you like to learn about this topic? Do you think you might learn about it from this book? Why or why not?*
5. *Use a reading journal to write about your knowledge of this topic. Record what you already know about the topic and what you hope to learn about the topic.*
6. *Read the book.*
7. *In your reading journal, record what you learned about the topic and your response to the book.*
8. *After reading the book complete the activities below.*

Content Area Vocabulary
Read the list. What do these words mean?

amphitheater
concrete
ellipse
engineers
excavated
foundation
gladiators
harbor
pontoons
retractable
spectators
stand
translucent
venue

After Reading:

Comprehension and Extension Activity

After reading the book, work on the following questions with your child or students in order to check their level of reading comprehension and content mastery.

1. *When was the first stadium built and what was it used for?* (Summarize)
2. *When creating a stadium, what other factors do engineers and designers need to consider?* (Infer)
3. *Why is stadium seating built in tiers?* (Asking questions)
4. *How have engineers created stadiums that benefit fans and adapt to the environment they are built in?* (Summarize)
5. *Have you been to a stadium? What unique features did you notice?* (Text to self connection)

Extension Activity
What is the closest stadium near you? What is it used for? How old is it? Does it have any unique features? Research a stadium near you and create a poster that gives information about your stadium. Present the information to your family and friends.

Table of Contents

Thousands of fans crowd into an enormous stadium to watch a soccer match under the bright lights.

All about Stadiums

Have you ever watched a live professional football game or rocked to your favorite band in concert? You probably watched these events in a stadium. A stadium is a structure where people watch sports competitions, music concerts, and other events. Participants play on a field or perform on a stage surrounded by **spectators**.

Brain Builder!

Another word for stadium is coliseum.

Think your school auditorium holds a lot of people? Stadiums are some of the biggest public structures in the world. Some stadiums have seats for more than 100,000 people. In fact, the largest stadium in the world is the Rungrado May Day Stadium in Pyongyang, North Korea. It seats 150,000 people!

Completed in 1989 and considered the largest stadium in the world, the Rungrado May Day Stadium in Pyongyang, North Korea, is used for a variety of events including soccer matches, sporting events, and festivals.

Most stadiums are built to host sporting events. In many places, professional sports teams partner with cities to build stadiums for baseball, football, and soccer teams. Colleges and universities build stadiums for their athletic teams. Governments also build stadiums for special events, such as the Olympic Games.

The city of London built the Olympic Stadium when it hosted the 2012 Summer Olympic Games. Beginning in 2016, the stadium will be used to host soccer matches, sporting events, and live music concerts.

Located in Arlington, Texas, AT&T Stadium is the home of the Dallas Cowboys, a National Football League team. Completed in 2009, it is considered the world's largest domed structure.

Building these super structures takes a lot of time, effort, and money. Stadium designs range from simple to complex. Building a stadium takes several years and hundreds of workers. Around the world, stadiums are some of the most amazing engineering wonders.

A tunnel-like entrance built with stone leads to the track in an early Greek stadium.

Early Greek Stadiums

More than 3,000 years ago, ancient Greeks built the first stadiums. The word stadium comes from the word *stadion*, an ancient Greek unit of length that equaled about 630 feet (192 meters).

The first stadiums had a simple, flat track in the arena. The track was made from hard-packed clay and shaped like a U. It had start and finish lines at the two ends.

A stone **stand** with separate entrances was built alongside the track. From the stands, judges and spectators could watch the athletes. Sometimes early stadiums were built near natural hills. Spectators could sit on the hill for a clear view of the races. Later, the Greeks added stone and marble seats to the stands. They also added steps and divisions to make it easier for spectators to enter and exit the seating area.

Spectators sat on hills and surrounding land to watch the races on the track in early Greek stadiums.

As sporting competitions became more popular, many Greek towns built stadiums. In the fourth century BCE, the Panathenaic Stadium was built in Athens, Greece. It was built in a small valley, between the two hills of Agra and Ardettos, over the Ilissos River. The stadium hosted athletic events for the Great Panathenaia, a celebration of the city of Athens. Every four years, these sporting games were held in honor of the Greek goddess Athena.

Brain Builder!

Ancient Greeks worshiped Athena, the goddess of war and wisdom. She became the patron goddess of the city of Athens after offering an olive tree to the Athenians.

Between 140 and 144 CE, Herodes Atticus renovated the Panathenaic Stadium. He gave the stadium its horseshoe shape and a track that measured 669 feet (204 meters) long and 272 feet (33 meters) wide. The stadium was covered in marble and seated approximately 50,000 people.

The people of Athens gathered at the Panathenaic Stadium to watch sporting events held in honor of the goddess Athena. It is the only stadium in the world built entirely of marble.

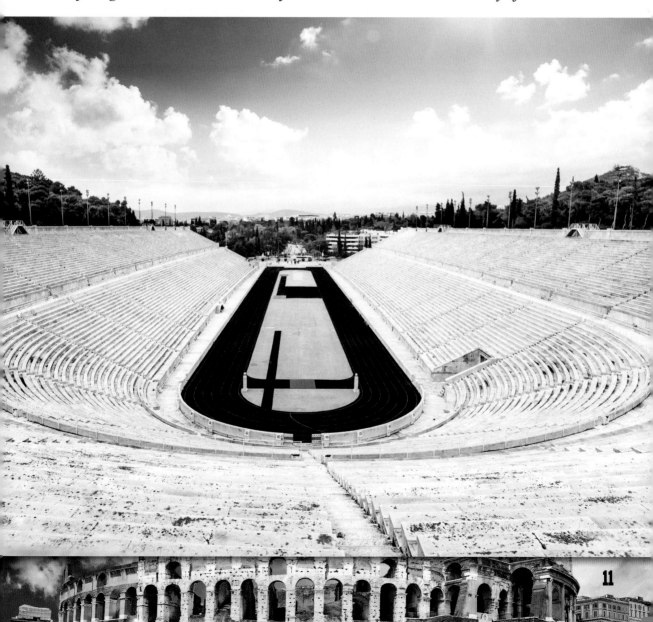

In 1896, spectators gathered to watch the first modern Olympic Games at the rebuilt Panathenaic Stadium.

During Roman times, **gladiators** fought in the stadium. A semi-circular wall was added to close the open northern end. During the Middle Ages, the stadium was not used and fell into disrepair.

In the 19th century, the remains of the ancient Panathenaic Stadium were **excavated** and rebuilt entirely with marble. Its track and design followed the ancient U-shaped form. Spectators sat on 50 rows of marble steps.

Brain Builder!

The Panathenaic Stadium is also known as the Kallimarmaro, which means "made of fine marble."

In 1896, the rebuilt Panathenaic Stadium hosted the first modern Olympic Games. The Games' opening and closing ceremonies were held in the stadium, along with competitions in athletics, gymnastics, weightlifting, and wrestling. The stadium also served as the finish line for the marathon race.

In 2004, the Olympic Games returned to Athens and Panathenaic Stadium. It hosted the archery competition. The stadium also served as the finish line for the women's and men's marathons. The stadium seated 45,000 people in rows of marble steps.

A Japanese fan waves a flag as he waits for the 2004 Olympic Games women's marathon athletes to enter the Panathenaic Stadium.

The original name of the Colosseum was the Flavian Amphitheater. It was named for the Flavius family name of Emperor Vespasian and his son Titus. Many people think that the name Colosseum came from a colossal statue of the Roman Emperor Nero outside the structure.

Rome's Coliseums

A ncient Romans built many stadiums to hold sporting competitions. One of the most famous was the Roman Colosseum, a massive stone **amphitheater**. In the first century CE, Rome's Emperor Vespasian ordered the construction of the amphitheater as a gift to the Roman people. It became the largest public entertainment **venue** in the Roman Empire. In 80 CE, the amphitheater opened with 100 days of games. Spectators watched gladiator matches and wild animal fights.

Circus Maximus

The Circus Maximus was a stadium built in Rome in the sixth century BCE. At the time, it was the biggest stadium ever built. The Circus was used for chariot races, as well as other public events, such as the Roman Games and gladiator fights. Spectator tiers were built on a natural slope. At first the stadium was built with wood. After several fires destroyed the wood structure, the Roman emperor had the Circus rebuilt in 103 CE with stone. The lower part of the seating area was built with marble. With the renovation, the Circus was more than 2,000 feet (600 meters) long and 50 feet (150 meters) wide. At its largest point in history, the Circus could hold 250,000 spectators. The last race at the Circus Maximus occurred in 549 CE. Today, it is one of Rome's important public spaces. It functions as a public park and hosts music concerts and rallies.

The Circus Maximus, located in the valley between the Palatine and Aventine hills, was originally built to host chariot races and the Roman Games to honor the Roman god Jupiter.

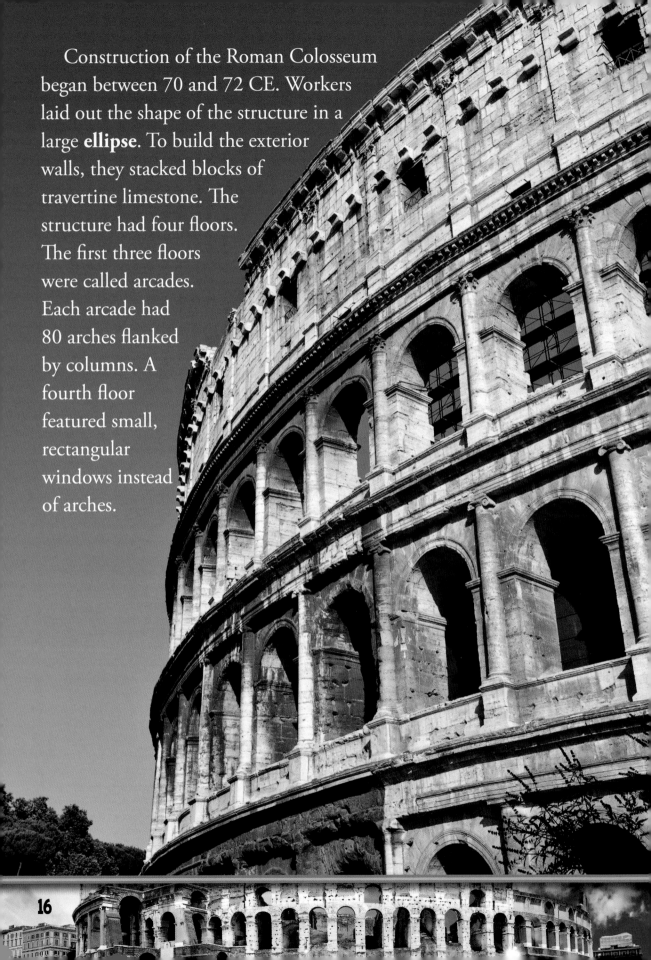

Construction of the Roman Colosseum began between 70 and 72 CE. Workers laid out the shape of the structure in a large **ellipse**. To build the exterior walls, they stacked blocks of travertine limestone. The structure had four floors. The first three floors were called arcades. Each arcade had 80 arches flanked by columns. A fourth floor featured small, rectangular windows instead of arches.

Most of the original Roman Colosseum has been destroyed, with only about one-third of the original amphitheater remaining. Much of the Colosseum's marble facing, statues, and interior decorations are gone.

The arena floor was made of wood, covered by a layer of sand. Below the arena floor, workers built a two-level basement called the hypogeum. The hypogeum was a maze of passages. It had an elaborate system of elevators, ramps, and trap doors to let gladiators and wild animals into the arena.

Brain Builder!

Like modern sports stadiums, the Roman Colosseum protected spectators from the hot Sun with an enormous canvas awning called a velarium. It hung by a system of ropes, winches, and wooden poles along the top of the stadium's outer wall. Many Roman sailors were needed to move it.

The Roman Colosseum could hold between 50,000 to 55,000 people, according to modern estimates.

Gladiators battle as spectators look on, cheering for their favorites.

Several types of events occurred at the Roman Colosseum. Some of the most popular were gladiator fights. Gladiators battled to the death for the crowd's entertainment. Animal hunts were also popular. These hunts frequently used elaborate scenery to recreate a realistic environment and imported animals from Africa and the Middle East.

After four centuries of use, the Colosseum fell into disrepair. People raided it for building materials. Over time, about two-thirds of the original structure was destroyed.

The Roman Colosseum is a popular tourist attraction in Rome. Nearly five million people visit it every year.

Located in Munich, Germany, Olympiastadion was the main venue for the 1972 Summer Olympic Games.

Modern Sports Marvels

Every year, millions of people visit sports stadiums to watch games, competitions, and other events. Large structures are needed to hold all of these people. Some of today's modern sports stadiums have gotten so big they can hold more than 100,000 people.

Although each stadium is unique, many modern stadiums share a similar structure. A strong steel or **concrete** frame rests on an underground **foundation**. The frame supports concrete slabs, which hold seating for thousands of people.

Many construction materials are used to build a modern stadium. Concrete and steel are typically used to build the foundation, frame, and roof. Other parts of a stadium are built with metals, bricks, stone, glass, and plastics.

Wembley Stadium

Wembley Stadium

Wembley Stadium is the second-largest stadium in Europe. It can hold 90,000 people. The current stadium opened in 2007 in London, England. It was constructed on the site of the old Wembley Stadium, which was built in 1924. Wembley is the home of the English national soccer team. It also hosts rugby matches, football games, track and field events, and music concerts.

Brain Builder!

Camp Nou in Barcelona, Spain, is the largest stadium in Europe. Built in the 1950s, it holds 99,786 fans and is home to the FC Barcelona soccer team.

Wembley is the tallest stadium in the world that covers every seat. The stadium's roof hangs from an arch that rises 436 feet (134 meters) over the stadium. The arch holds up part of the roof's weight. This allows the stadium to not use pillars that would block the fans' view of the field. The roof is partially **retractable**. It can be opened to let in sunlight for the stadium's grass field. It can also be closed so that every seat is covered.

Did You Know?

Wembley has 2,618 toilets, more than any venue in the world.

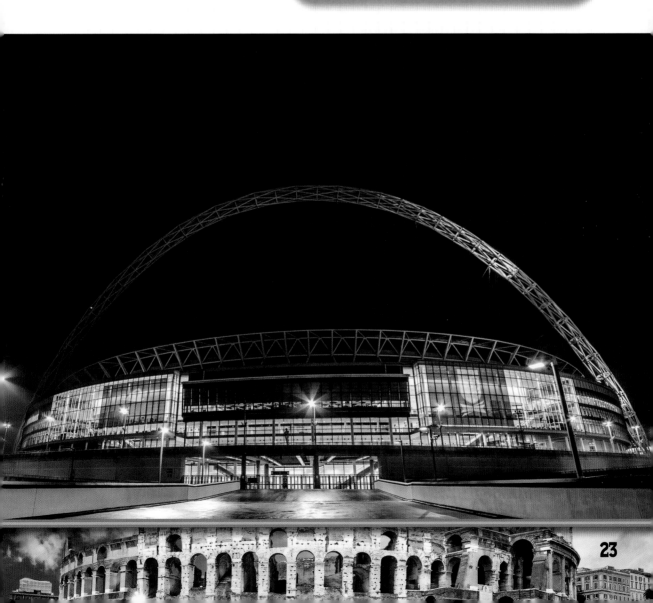

The stands at The Float at Marina Bay in Singapore's harbor can hold 30,000 fans.

The Float at Marina Bay

Singapore is one of the world's most crowded countries. There is not a lot of space to build a large stadium. To solve the problem, **engineers** came up with an interesting solution. They built the stadium stands next to Singapore's **harbor**. The field of the stadium, however, floats over the harbor's waters. This makes The Float at Marina Bay the largest floating stadium in the world.

The stadium's floating platform is made entirely of steel. It measures 394 feet (120 meters) long and 272 feet (83 meters) wide. The floating platform can hold up to 1,179 tons (1,070 metric tons). That is the same amount of weight as about 780 mid-size cars. The stadium's field floats on top of 15 **pontoons**. Its surface is covered with artificial turf.

Completed in 2007, the floating stadium is a multi-purpose facility. It is used for spectator events, sporting events, and cultural performances.

Fireworks explode over The Float at Marina Bay as spectators watch performances for the National Day Parade.

Rungrado May Day Stadium hosts football matches and other sporting events. It is the world's largest stadium for capacity, or the number of people it holds. It is the world's 12th largest sporting venue.

Rungrado May Day Stadium

Rungrado May Day Stadium in Pyongyang, North Korea, is the largest stadium in the world. It was built to host the 13th World Festival of Youth and Students in 1989. It seats 150,000 people, and sometimes it holds even more. During May Day holiday shows, thousands of dancers, gymnasts, and other performers are in the building. Some of these shows use as many as 100,000 performers. Altogether, there can be more than 200,000 people in the stadium at the same time!

The stadium hosts a variety of sporting and cultural events. It was designed with eight floors and a main floor space of more than 2.2 million square feet (207,000 square meters). The stadium is equipped for almost every sport. It has an indoor swimming pool, training halls, a 400-meter track, and a 242,200 square foot (22,500 square meter) field. Today, the stadium is mainly used for festival events, dance performances and soccer matches.

Thousands of performers fill Rungrado May Day Stadium and perform gymnastic and artistic routines to celebrate North Korea's Arirang festival.

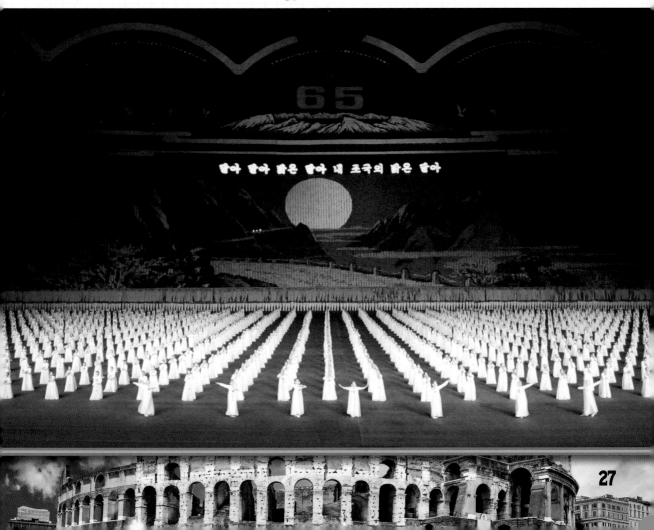

Athletes celebrate Madaraka Day in Nyayo National Stadium. Madaraka Day celebrates the beginning of Kenya's independence from Britain.

Nyayo National Stadium

Nyayo National Stadium is a multi-purpose stadium in Kenya. Built in 1983, the stadium is located near the city center of Nairobi, Kenya's capital. The stadium holds 30,000 people and is the second largest stadium in Kenya. It frequently hosts professional soccer games and is the home of the All Footballers' Confederation (AFC) Leopards Sports Club.

The stadium is a full-featured sports complex. A running track surrounds the main field. It also has an aquatic center with an Olympic-sized pool, an indoor gymnasium, and arena that can be used for volleyball, wrestling, and other sporting events. The stadium hosts the AFC Leopards soccer team, a member of the Kenyan Premier League. It also is the headquarters for the Kenya Football Federation. It has been used for several important sporting events, including the 2010 African Championships in Athletics. In addition, the stadium's main field is frequently used for large public gatherings such as outdoor conferences and political events.

Athletes compete in a race for Nairobi's Olympic Trials in 2012 in preparation for the 2012 London Summer Olympics.

The Toronto Blue Jays of Major League Baseball play in the Rogers Centre, formerly known as the Toronto SkyDome.

Flexible Stadiums

Engineers design some stadiums with moving parts. These structures have roofs that can retract and fields that can move. These flexible stadiums can change at a moment's notice.

Brain Builders!

In 1989, Toronto, Canada, opened the SkyDome. It was the first stadium built with a fully retractable roof.

The SkyDome's roof can open or close in 20 minutes.

The Houston Texans and the Jacksonville Jaguars, play under the lights of NRG Stadium in Houston, Texas.

NRG Stadium

NRG Stadium in Houston, Texas, is the first stadium to have a natural grass playing field and a retractable roof. NRG Stadium is home to the National Football League's Houston Texans and the Houston Livestock Show and Rodeo.

The designers of NRG Stadium wanted to build a stadium with a natural grass playing field to take advantage of Houston's year-round sunshine. They also wanted to protect the field and spectators from Houston's unpredictable weather. To solve this problem, the designers created a retractable roof for the stadium. The roof can be opened in good weather and closed in bad weather.

NRG Stadium can seat 71,500 fans.

The stadium roof consists of two large panels that separate over the 50-yard line. The panels are made of fiberglass fabric, a very lightweight material. The two panels slide apart along a set of tracks. They lie over each end zone when fully retracted. Roof operation is controlled in the stadium press box using a computer.

In August 2013, NRG Stadium unveiled 14,549 square feet (1,352 square meters) of video screens in the stadium's end zones, the largest digital displays in any professional sports venue.

The roof can be opened or closed in as little as seven minutes. The roof's panels move at a speed of up to 35 feet (11 meters) per minute. The roof can be opened or closed in winds up to 50 miles (80 kilometers) per hour.

On hot or rainy days, NRG Stadium's retractable roof can be closed to protect fans and the field.

The University of Phoenix Stadium's moveable field supports approximately 94,000 square feet (8,247 square meters) of natural grass.

University of Phoenix Stadium

Many football players prefer to play on grass fields. Grass is softer than artificial turf on players' feet and legs. It is not easy, however, to grow grass inside a stadium. The University of Phoenix Stadium was designed to look like a barrel cactus wrapped by a snake. The design did not allow enough sunlight in to support a natural grass field. The University of Phoenix Stadium came up with a creative way to solve this problem. They moved the grass field outside the stadium!

The stadium's field sits on a moveable floor. A nearly 19 million pound (8.6 million kilogram) tray holds 92,000 square feet (8,247 square meters) of grass, drainage, and an irrigation system. The 40 inch (101 centimeter) deep tray rests on 13 railroad-like tracks. Most of the time, the field tray stays outside the stadium, allowing the grass to grow in sunlight. For games, the field slides back inside the stadium. It moves through an opening by the end zone on the stadium's southeastern end. The tray moves in and out of the stadium on 42 rows of steel wheel assemblies. It takes about an hour for the tray to move 741 feet (226 meters).

The grass field remains outside the stadium in the Sun until game day, getting the maximum amount of sunshine and nourishment.

The unique structure of Beijing's Bird's Nest is covered with a polymer membrane, which allows it to glow at night when lit inside.

Urban Icons

Some stadiums are recognized around the world for their interesting appearance. These stadiums look like nothing else in the world.

Beijing National Stadium

In 2008, China hosted the Olympic Games. To prepare for the events, the country held a competition to see who could design the best new stadium. Swiss architects Jacques Herzog and Pierre de Meuron and Chinese architect Li Xinggang won the competition. They created the Beijing National Stadium. The 91,000-seat stadium was designed to incorporate elements of Chinese art and culture. The stadium's unique design looks like a jumble of exposed steel twigs. With its oval shape and twisted steel sides, it quickly became known as the Bird's Nest.

The Bird's Nest is the world's largest steel structure. It is also one of the most complex stadiums ever built. To build the stadium, large tubes of steel were twisted around one another to create the nest-like shape. The stadium used 42,000 tons (38,102 metric tons) of steel. The stadium stretches 1,093 feet (333 meters) by 965 feet (294 meters). It soars 226 feet (69 meters) tall.

Builders used the purest steel ever developed in China to build the Bird's Nest. The steel is lightweight but also strong enough to resist potential earthquakes.

The Bird's Nest hosted the opening ceremony, several athletic events, and the closing ceremonies for the 2008 Beijing Summer Olympics.

The Bird's Nest was built to withstand earthquakes. During an earthquake, the shaking ground can damage or destroy a building if it is not flexible enough to absorb the movement. To protect the Bird's Nest, the structure was built in two parts – the concrete bowl and the steel structure. In addition, the spectator stands were built in eight zones, each with its own stability system. If one zone moves during an earthquake, it will not affect other zones. This design allows the stadium to absorb the Earth's movement during an earthquake.

Sustainable Features

The Bird's Nest was designed for environmental sustainability. It has an open roof, which allows for natural airflow and natural light. Natural light also enters through a **translucent** membrane that is wrapped around the building. These features reduce the need for large electrical systems.

A rainwater collection system conserves water and saves energy. The water is used in the stadium's bathrooms and to irrigate the field. The designers also put special pipes under the stadium's field. The pipes gather heat from the Earth in the winter and cold in the summer. This allows the stadium to control its temperature naturally.

Rainwater collection systems can be used in many buildings, from small residential homes to large stadiums like the Bird's Nest.

Allianz Arena's outer shell is lit by 1,056 illuminated panels, with each panel containing four individual lights.

Allianz Arena

The Allianz Arena in Munich, Germany, can change colors with the press of a button. Opened in 2005, the stadium holds about 70,000 people and is home to the Bayern Munich and TSV 1860 Munich soccer clubs.

The color of the stadium changes based on the team that's playing. The stadium's luminous exterior is covered with 2,874 clear plastic panels. These panels are inflated with air. They provide insulation to the structure. They also make the stadium look like a huge spacecraft. To make the stadium change colors, lighting tubes shine filtered light through the plastic. Changing the filter changes the color of the light visible through the panels.

Allianz Arena is the first stadium in the world that can change colors, with its entire outer facade able to illuminate in red, white, or blue.

Timeline

Sixth century BCE – The Circus Maximus is built in Rome, the biggest stadium of the time.

Fourth century BCE – The original Panathenaic Stadium is built in Athens, Greece.

80 CE – The Roman Colosseum opens for 100 days of games.

1896 – The rebuilt Panathenaic Stadium hosts the first modern Olympic Games.

1908 – London's White City Stadium hosts the 1908 Olympic Games and is considered to be the first modern era sports stadium.

1964 – Shea Stadium opens in New York as the world's first multi-use stadium.

1965 – The Astrodome in Houston, Texas, opens as the first large indoor stadium.

1989 – The first retractable roof on the Toronto SkyDome debuts.

2005 – Allianz Arena opens and changes color based on the team that is playing.

2007 – The rebuilt Wembley Stadium opens in London, England.

2007 – The world's largest floating stadium, The Float at Marina Bay, opens.

2008 – Beijing, China, hosts the Olympic Games and impresses the world with Beijing National Stadium's design.

Glossary

amphitheater (AM-fi-thee-uh-tur): a large, open-air building with rows of seats in high circles around an arena

concrete (KON-kreet): a very hard material made from cement, water, and aggregate

ellipse (i-LIPS): an oval shape

engineers (en-juh-NEERS): people who design and build structures

excavated (EK-skuh-vate-ed): carefully dug out and removed ancient remains

foundation (foun-DEY-shuhn): underground part of a building that supports the weight of the building

gladiators (GLAD-ee-ey-ters): people who fought to the death for public entertainment in Ancient Rome

harbor (HAR-bur): an area of water where ships load and unload goods

pontoons (pon-TOONZ): floating structures that are used to support things on water

retractable (ri-TRAKT-uh-buhl): able to be moved back and forth

spectators (SPEK-tay-turz): people watching athletic contests, concerts, or other events

stand (STAND): an area of raised seating from which spectators watch the action in a stadium

translucent (transs-LOO-suhnt): allowing some light to pass through

venue (VEN-yoo): a place where an event is held

Index

Show What You Know

1. Why was the original Panathenaic Stadium built?
2. How was the Roman Colosseum used?
3. How many spectators can fit into Rungrado May Day Stadium?
4. What problem does a retractable roof solve?
5. Why is the Beijing National Stadium easily recognized?

Websites to Visit

www.worldstadiums.com

www.si.com/nfl/2015/01/29/super-bowl-xlix-university-of-phoenix-
    stadium-glendale-turf

www.history.com/topics/ancient-history/colosseum

About the Author

Carla Mooney has written many books for children and young adults. She lives in Pennsylvania with her husband and three children. She enjoys learning about world history and has been to several stadiums to watch professional football and baseball games and concerts.

Meet The Author!
www.meetREMauthors.com

PHOTO CREDITS: Cover ©Marius GODOI; title page © efks; page top © Zheka-Boss; page 4 © Aksonov; page 5 © Nyiragongo70; page 6 © Johnny Greig; page 7 © wellesenterprises; page 8 © alxpin; page 9 © Afagundes; page 10 © dimitriosp; page 11 © Sergey Novikov/ripicts.com; page 12 © Tim Hawkins/ Eye Ubiquitous; page 13 © Lefteris Pitarakis/AP; page 14 © freeartist; page 15 © Francesco Contone Udokant; page 16 © btrenkel; page 17 © Barry Kearney; page 18 © North Wind Pictures Archives; page 19 © marek Slusarczyk; page 20 © Dmitry V. Petrenko; page 21 © Rafal Olkis, Olha Rohulya; page 22 © Rcavalleri, Iakov Filimonov; page 23 © Zefart; page 24 © joyfull; page 25 © Jordan Tan; page 26btrenkel; page 27 © Wanghanan; page 28 © Daniel Irungu/Corbis; page 29 © Demotix/De Mattei; page 30 © Maurizio De Mattei; page 31 © Ravitt75; page 32 © Baronoskie; page 33 © Tor3685; page 34 © urban houstonian; page 35 © Ed Schipul; page 36 © Imdan; page 37 © Kiz28; page 38 © Sihasakprachum; page 39 © Ma Liang; page 40 © Photonphotos; page 41 © Zstockphotos; page 42 © Ralf Hettler; page 43 © Yorgy67

Edited by: Keli Sipperley

Cover and interior design by: Renee Brady

Library of Congress PCN Data

Stadiums and Coliseums / Carla Mooney
(Engineering Wonders)
ISBN 978-1-63430-417-7 (hard cover)
ISBN 978-1-63430-517-4 (soft cover)
ISBN 978-1-63430-608-9 (e-Book)
Library of Congress Control Number: 2015931730

Also Available as:
ROURKE'S e-Books

Printed in the United States of America, North Mankato, Minnesota